I TRIED TO
STAY OUT OF
THIS.
BUT ITS SO
CORNY THIS
KID'S I

THINK HE THINKS
THAT BEING AGAINST
THE LIBERALS
MAKES IT'S U BE PUNK

IF
IT'S
YOU.

ISN'T EVERYONE
STUPID COMPARED

YOUR FRIEND

SEEING WAY MORE 2 LEGGED DOGS THESE DAYS.

TWO COPS ARE STANDING OVER A CURLED FIGURE [SIC] IN THE ▲ LOWER DEPTHS. LIT BY FILAMENTS OF LIGHT / ENTOMBED IN THE SLUICE OF BLOOD. SILT + SEDIMENT ⊠ ⊠. PINK FLECKS OF EMBROIDERY. THE ALTAR CUT FROM A DIORITE POMMELHORSE. MUSCLES STILL [CONT]

BULBOUS & QUIVERING. STIFFENING INTO TIGHT BUSHELS. *THE BODY FULL OF THIS & ONLY HUNGER.*

– – – – – – – – – – – – –

THEY ARE STANDING OVER ↓ THE CORPSE OF A SMALL ANIMAL. A RACOON OR POSSUM OR DOG. SOMETHING WITH COARSE HAIR + LARGE GASHES

ACROSS ITS STOMACH. MILK DRIPPING THRU ITS EYES. *HIS MOST RECENT OBLITERATION.* DRAGGED FROM THE SURFACE BACK INTO THE ▲ SUBTERRANEAN. RENDERED OUT AS A FAWNING TAPESTRY. THE DISCOLORATIONS OF THE BARE SKIN TURNED [SIC] PAINTERLY W/ SOFT

WATERCOLORS.
[…] THEY ARE TALKING
ABOUT A SERIES OF ⊠
⊠ CODED MESSAGES—
**MAYBE SOMETHING
MAYBE NOTHING**
[*PROJECTION-1*] A PICKET /
A DEMONSTRATION /
BOMB / PUBLIC WERKS.
A GESTURAL EVENT. THE
FIRST LEANS CLOSE TO
THE CORPSE & SAYS,

I AM A HUMAN BOMB. THE SECOND STAYS BACK & SAYS HE HOPES THE NOTHING IS SOMETHING

- - - - - - - - - - - - -

[...] HE REMOVES AN ORNAMENTAL KNIFE FROM HIS BELT & LINES IT OVER THE CENTER OF THE CADAVER. HE SAYS THE CENTER OF THE CADAVER IS A SITE OF

DIVINATION ▲ [CONT]
A GOOD INCISION CAN
CREATE A THRESHOLD
FOR DESIRES TO → PASS
THRU. HIS DESIRE IS TO
WITNESS A FIRE IN THE
COMMUNITY GARDEN,
OR A NEW TORSO
SEVERED & LEVITATING,
DRIPPING ITS GUTS
INTO THE RIVER. THE
SOUND OF WAILING

CHILDREN. HE THINKS, *THERE WILL ALWAYS BE MORE PEOPLE.* MORE CONTOURS TO READ. SCENES TO DISLODGE. *YOU DO WHAT YOU WILL & AT THE END FANON'S GHOST WILL BE WAITING FOR YOU.* [...] SO MANY BODIES ALL AT ONCE & YR EYES ARE STILL → THERE. ☒ ☒ ☒ ☒ WAITING

IN THE DARK OF THE ALCOVES AS THEY SHIFT FROM CONCRETE TO PITCH. THE KNIFE SINKS INTO THE SALLOW MEAT, & YOU WATCH IT SHAPE A MAZE OF INTRICATE PATTERNS. LONG STROKES THAT CURL & INTERSECT TOWARDS THE CENTER BEFORE PROLIFERATING

OUTWARDS INTO WINDING PATHS THAT EVENTUALLY FOLD BACK INTO THE ANIMAL'S ANATOMY [*PROJECTION-2*] THRU THE OPENING. THRU THE MAW. FURLS OF MUSCLE, FAT, ▲ THE OLD-FASHIONED FLESH READ AS SACRED GLYPHS. DRAGGING LANGUAGE FROM THE

MUTILATED REMAINS OF THE BODY. HE SAYS, *WE ARE SCRYING A DIVINE LAW FROM THE LAMB-THAT-IS-NOT-A-LAMB.* PREPARING A FEAST ▲ FROM THE TEXT […] A TALISMAN IS NOT MADE REAL [SIC] THRU ITS CONSTRUCTION, BUT THRU THE ARCANE INTENSITIES THAT IMBUE

IT → IN THIS WAY, THE POLICE DO NOT VALUE THE DEATH OF THE BODY, BUT THE CREATION OF THE CADAVER. ☒ ☒ ☒

- - - - - - - - - - - - - -

DEVOURED OR W / O DEPTH 📇 & FROM THE SLIT, DEMONS / SCABS / LITURGIES. *WHAT OPENS A HUMAN BEING* [SIC] THE HOLY

FETISHES. A CATHEDRAL FORMED BY THE DARK ALCOVES OF THE CAVE / SEWERS / WHEREVER WE ARE NOW. IN THE PRESENCE OF THE ☒ ☒ ☒ PIGFLESH. A SERMON DEMONSTRATED BY DISEMBODIED VOICES & SEVERED HANDS. [CONT] GESTURES THAT ALLUDE TO → ANOTHER

ASSASSINATION ATTEMPT. A MOSAIC OF EMBROIDERED HANDGUNS [*PROJECTION-3*]. EXPERIMENTAL STATE-BUILDING. WHATEVER SERIES OF EVENTS MIGHT BE USED TO JUSTIFY A RESPONSE ‼ [...] THRU THE CURTAINS OF THE WOUND. UNDER THE SLIT-TONGUE.

POUR OUT YR ANGUISH! [FRTHR DWN] ANOTHER BODY / ANOTHER BOMB. I AM A HUMAN BOMB IN THE BOAT OF RA. ABLAZE WITH ASBESTOS FUMES. ⊠ ⊠ CURLING & FLAILING THRU THE THICK AIR OF THE ▲ SUBTERRANEAN. BTWN THIS MIASMA & THE NEXT […] THE TWO COPS LOOK INTO THE

OPEN WOUND AND THEY SEE SCABS SWARMED IN HALF-DECAYED MURMURATIONS ☒ ☒. FLOODING THE PIPELINE. PUTTING OUT THE FIRES OF ANOTHER BURNING OIL RIG. *IT IS BEST TO ARTICULATE YR VIOLENCE OFF-SHORE.* [*PROJECTION-4*] → AT SITES OF ▲ PARTICULAR

GEOPOLITICAL INTENSITY & AFFECT [*PROJECTION-5*] THERE IS A MOUNTING TENSION HERE, BTWN THE HORSE-FACE & THE OX-MASK. THE TWO COPS ○ ARE DRESSED IN ANIMAL COSTUMES. FOUL SKULLS ◌ OVER THEIR HEADS, HARSH-CUT FURS DRAPED OVER THEIR TORSOS. [CONT] ⊜ IT IS

BETTER TO SEE RITUAL THRU THE EYES OF THE VICTIM. WITHOUT THAT [SIC] PRIMITIVE URGE TO CREATE CORPSES. TO SEE WHAT THE CADAVER SEES. TO FEEL THAT SAME FEAR WHEN THE KNIFE FIRST ✋ TOUCHES YR STOMACH. READY TO UNSEW SOMETHING HELPLESS & OPEN A

PORTAL TO HELL.

[…] WHAT IS DIVINATED FROM ↓ THE MUTILATED REMAINS CANNOT BE KNOWN UNTIL THE ACT IS COMPLETE. ▲ IT IS ONLY AFTER THE BOMB HAS DETONATED THAT ITS INDICTMENT CAN BE ATTRIBUTED TO THE RITUAL. ⊠ ⊠ AFTER

EVERY CONSPIRATOR / WITNESS / VICTIM HAS BEEN CAPTURED. THEY → CAN THEN HOLD UP THE CADAVER & SAY, [SIC] *WE KNOW THIS WAS YOU. WE SEE WHAT YOU'VE DONE.* THE BODY CONDEMNS ITS SUBJECT & FROM IT, THESE NEW VESSELS MAY BE USED TO FORSEE FURTHER EVENTS → THE

FUTURE IS RENDERED ACTUAL THRU THE DESECRATION OF STATE-PROCURED BODIES ▲ [*BECOMING-CADAVER*]. THE LAMB-THAT-IS-NOT-A-LAMB. TURNED INSIDE-OUT TO BE READ AS THE SCENES ON AN URN. EACH DEMARCATION OF THE FLESH, A NEW WRIT OF DEVOTION ‼

TO BE USED AGAINST CORPSES STILL TO COME / STIGMATA YET TO SURFACE […]

THE LITTLE MARSHES BTWN ○ & ● WHERE THE LOWER HALF OF YOUR HEAD LIES DORMANT.

INSIDE OF THE BODY IS

ANOTHER BODY / INSIDE THE SKULL ANOTHER SKULL [...] SOMETHING OF SIMILAR DIMENSIONS, STRUCTURE, COMPOSITION, THAT CAN BE EXTRACTED THRU THE GULLET AND LAID ACROSS THE ALTAR. THE INTERIOR CORRODED BY A FORM OUTSIDE OF LANGUAGE [...]

ELOAK

www.ingramcontent.com/pod-product-compliance
Ingram Content Group UK Ltd.
Pitfield, Milton Keynes, MK11 3LW, UK
UKHW042000230426
12048UKWH00009B/437